Living Through the Aftermath

Jonnetta "Jai" Allen

Copyright © 2014 Jonnetta "Jai" Allen

All rights reserved.

ISBN: 0615985696
ISBN-13: 978-0615985695

DEDICATION

To my children: Tajhinea & D'Maje... Please always remember that the sky is not the limit when there are footprints on the moon.

This book is dedicated to any person that has ever gone through anything that rocked their very existence. Afterwards, they had no idea how they would pick up the pieces and/or move on. This book is for you. Just know this if you don't get anything else from this experience: if you're going through it, it's because you can handle it. This is not the last stop for you. Keep going you're only passing through. It's darkest before dawn. It will work out for your good. I promise.

Blessings

ACKNOWLEDGMENTS

First, I have to acknowledge God who is the very source of my existence. When I didn't feel like going on, it was you Lord who carried me. You not only carried me, but you kept my mind! God, I thank and praise you! I recognize that I don't know where I would be if it were not for you.

To my husband, Kenneth Holmes, I had no idea life would go this way. It has, and as much as I don't understand, I'm grateful. In this journey, I'm learning to just be the best that I could be, and be content with that. My best isn't always going to be good enough for everyone. Hopefully, one day you'll read these pages, and agree with me that I was in fact, the best wife I could possibly be. I love you.

Mom, (Ya Ya) there really are no words that can adequately depict who you are and what you do. I simply want to thank you. Dad, thank you! My favorite uncle in America.... I love you! Pastor (Dad) & Mrs. Treadwell (mom), thank you for being there and loving on me. I received a strong spiritual foundation, and I am eternally grateful!

Jay, my best everything! Who knew? Certainly I didn't. But the one thing I do know is that God does all things well, and for this friendship I'm thankful. You push me and challenge me in ways that I never thought possible. You've walked with me, and there aren't many I can say that about. Thank you so much. Love you from the east to the west!

Mia X, watching your transition has been encouraging. If the only person this journey for was you, then I am still eternally grateful. Once your wings were ready, you never stopped flying. Don't ever get tired.

Aunt Cyndi, words don't even come close to describing the love you show me. I love you!

Viviana & Starski, what do I say to you? Right when I'm in need, you always show up. I haven't forgotten you Darling ViVi. Thank you for your friendship. Star, you challenged me to let people in to my world, and well here it is. Thank you!

To everyone who has uttered any words of encouragement to me in this particular season of my life, thank you!

If I have forgotten anyone please charge it to my head and not my heart...

I'm still growing

Invitation: Live Purposefully Through the Aftermath

In this journal, I hope to challenge you to change your perspectives. Sometimes we can become so engulfed in the things that are going wrong, that we often miss the things that are going right. Most often there is a person somewhere, believe it or not, that is worse off than you. So please take this journey with an open heart, and watch things change.

In 1 Kings 18, there is a story of a famine in the land. Elijah asked God to send rain. God said that He would. Elijah sent a servant out to see if there were clouds. The servant went out and came back and said he didn't see anything. Elijah told him to look again. I can only imagine what was going through his mind. Perhaps it was the premise that God said He would, He cannot lie, so the rain has to come. God never said when He would send it, just that He would send it. It was perhaps Elijah's response along with his faith. The servant went to look again on seven different occasions. The 7th time, the servant came back saying, "well there's a cloud, but it doesn't look like it will produce rain. Elijah began to praise God. The rain came. My point is: just because something doesn't look the way you think it's supposed to look, or things don't turn out the way you thought they would, doesn't mean the blessing isn't there. Look again.

There's a story that goes something like this: life is full of hard situations, which is like getting thrown into a pot of boiling water. There are three ways you can choose to react. You can react like a carrot, an egg or a tea bag. The carrot seems strong, hard and unrelenting at first, but when thrown in hot water, it becomes weak and soft. With adversity it loses its strength, and is able to bend in any direction. The egg is fragile. Its thin outer shell protects its liquid interior. But after sitting through the boiling water (adversity), the liquid interior hardens and cannot be changed afterwards. The shell (outward appearance) looks the same, but when broken, the hardness will still be there.

The tea bag is different than the carrot and the egg. Once it gets placed in hot water, it releases flavor and fragrance to everything else in the pot. It changes the water. As situations get worse, the tea bag continuously gets better and it changes the situation. So let me ask you: how do you handle adversity? Do you get soft like a carrot, hard like an egg, or are you strong like a tea bag? Think about it. I pray that by the time you finish this journal, you will be encouraged and motivated to be a tea bag. Sometimes God may use hot water to reveal who you really are. I'm learning more and more, that praise is the prayer that changes everything.

"More than most, I know the pain of surviving, after all, dying isn't like living; it requires no effort at all." –Ann Aguirre

Being able to stand tall and sift through the debris that has mostly been cleared away, and you're still there sniffing and searching for the pieces of yourself that got hurt. Can you imagine? The divorce is final, you lost your job, you receive unemployment or found a new job, you can move on with your life, but you're still trying to cope with the aftermath. The dictionary defines the aftermath as a period immediately following a usually ruinous event; the consequence of a situation, often one that is destructive. Now the level of destruction or ruin will not be the same for everyone. Your situation might be rape, abuse, failed marriage, drug addiction, eviction, abortion etc., but there's hope for you. You can get past the wreckage. Your recovery is waiting for you. Move forward.

Some of you are saying: Jai, you don't understand. I've been through hell or I'm going through hell. I hear you, but the key word is "through". That word depicts movement. Keep walking, you don't have to dwell there. The truth is that everything you've been through serves a purpose. Good, bad or indifferent, there was a lesson to be learned. So let's take this journey together, and prayerfully you'll be blessed through this process. I pray that you will be encouraged. Your process won't be like mine, but keep going.

Expect God to do it!

"Now unto Him who is able to do exceeding abundantly above all we can ask or think, according to the power that works within us." Ephesians 3:20

Day 1: Keep Calm… I'm expecting God to do it! It's not for me to say what "it" is. I just know that there isn't anything that God cannot do. I'm expecting Him to do miraculous things in your life from this moment on. All you need to do is have faith the size of a mustard seed and believe. So tell me: What are you expecting God to do?

Journal Writing:

_____
_____
_____
_____
_____
_____
_____
_____
_____
_____

Living Through the Aftermath

Caterpillar, your wings are ready

Day 2: Some of you may be familiar with the process that a caterpillar goes through to transition to a butterfly. We always marvel at the beauty of a butterfly, but do we ever wonder what it went through? The caterpillar had to fight to come out of the cocoon. And sometimes, depending on how observant you are, you may stumble upon it in the midst of its transition. The natural thing to do, if you see it struggling is to help it. But helping it can kill it. Apply it to yourself. You have to fight through certain circumstances in order that you might become all that God desires for you to become. And you may reach out to people for help and even get angry because they won't help. Perhaps God is preventing them from helping you. The process can't be sped up, and you cannot receive any assistance because it can kill you. Don't forfeit the process. You've come too far. I know it's hard. I know you think you won't make it. But you will. I can hear God saying: your time as a caterpillar has expired. Your wings are ready. Think of the last situation you thought you weren't going to make it through… You're still here, even though you can't see your way. God's got you. Keep going.

Journal Writing: Reflect on a situation, that while you were going through it you didn't see how you would make it? Look at where you are now? What situation are you in that it seems you won't make it? Tell God about it.

_____

_____

_____

_____

_____

_____

_____

_____

Living Through the Aftermath

What Does God Say?

Day 3: He said, she said, we said, they said, I said… But what does God say? It doesn't matter to me what people are saying about you. Honestly, if they're talking behind your back, 9 times out of 10 you're too far ahead of them for them to say it to you. Not that it doesn't hurt, but does it really matter? Are they providing for you?

I'm sure you can tell me all the negative things others have said about you and/or things that you have said about and to yourself.

Journal Writing: Write 10 things about you, that you absolutely adore about yourself. And then pay it forward by complimenting someone else.
Who did you compliment? What did you say and how did they react/respond?

_____
_____
_____
_____
_____
_____
_____
_____
_____
_____
_____
_____
_____

Living Through the Aftermath

Confront It!

"Be subject, then, to God; stand up against the devil, and he will flee from you." James 4:7

Day 4: Let me get this out of the way and I'm pretty sure that you will come back to this day quite a bit. As you draw closer to God, the enemy is going to come harder. The Bible says to confront the enemy and he will flee. He has to. So I wrote him a letter:

Dear Satan:
I'm a little upset that I allowed you to ruffle my feathers today. I should've known that you were coming for me, after embarking on this journey. But I wasn't focused so you got me. To make it so bad, you don't even have any new tricks. But I've got my bearings and I'm focused. I always know when I'm close to my breakthrough because you raise your head. But I'm serving you notice: you have until I finish writing this, to vacate the premises or I will be forced to take action. Oh! And if that was your best shot, you've got to come better than that! The Bible says if confronted you will flee. So consider yourself served, confronted or whatever. I'm telling you to keep it moving, because this ain't what you want. Legal action is next: I WILL GET ON MY KNEES!
Sincerely,
Not Easily Broken

Write your own personal letter to Satan.

_____

_____

_____

_____

_____

_____

_____

_____

Living Through the Aftermath

It Will Work Out!

"And we know that all things work together for the good to them that love God and are the called according to His purpose." Romans 8:28

Day 5: You may not see it right now, but it's working for your good. You may not understand it right now, but it's working for your good. God will give you favor even after a failure. It's working for your good. He's allowing you to go through it because He knows you can handle it. This is not the end for you. Live through it.

Journal Writing: What are you living through?

_____
_____
_____
_____
_____
_____
_____
_____
_____
_____
_____
_____
_____

Living Through the Aftermath

Free Yourself!

{singing} Pain and pressures all around, cares they try to hold me down. But I stand in liberty and suddenly I'm free, suddenly I'm free, suddenly I'm free and suddenly I'm Free!

Day 6: I refuse to be held captive any longer. What about you? "This" has taken up too much time. Whatever happened, however drastic or whatever it didn't kill me. Guess what? You're reading this so it didn't kill you either. In fact, it strengthened me, and I hope you'll learn to see the strength you acquired because of it. The word heroine was on my mind. So I looked it up… Heroine (it should have said your name) but it said a woman of distinguished courage or ability, admired for her brave deeds and noble qualities. The bottom line is every one of us faces challenges. You have the power to determine how you react. It may knock you down but it's up to you to stay down or get back up, dust off and try again. The person, who has never achieved success, is the person who chose to stay down. I don't know what your challenges are, but if you're reading this, it's not the end of your story. You are in fact a heroine! Dust yourself off and figure out how to get back in there. I'm thankful today for this process. Begin to talk with people about things or learn to listen and really hear when people speak with you. You'll find that what they're speaking to you about is part of your story and they don't even know it. Share. People are watching what you do and listening to what you say. Do and say things on purpose! You may impact, change or save a life.

Journal Writing: Free yourself of some things... I'm listening

_____

_____

_____

_____

_____

_____

Believe God

Day 7: Have you ever been the event coordinator of your own pity party? I was. I didn't invite anyone because I had no need to. I questioned my integrity, intelligence and my worth. I wondered if I would ever be loved with the same intensity, and at the same capacity that I give it. You ever been there? I had to begin to speak over myself. At the end of the day it doesn't matter. Neither you nor I are responsible for other people. But we have to take full responsibility for ourselves. I plan to love as hard and as intentionally as I can. When it's all said and done, it doesn't matter what anyone else knows: I know that I gave it all that I've got. My pain had/has a purpose. I don't know who's affected by my story/experiences until they tell me. But if it's only for one person He's already done enough. So to that I say thank you Lord for all you've done for me! Are things great? No! But I'm still standing. I survived! I'm alive! And so are you! There's a reason. Don't suffer in silence. Someone needs your story. I don't care what the problem is, every day is a struggle. But now unto Him who is able to do exceeding abundantly above all that we can ask or think.

Journal Writing: I am standing with you. What are we believing God to do?

_____

_____

_____

_____

_____

_____

_____

Living Through the Aftermath

THEY THAT WAIT...

"Yet those who wait for the Lord will gain new strength; they will mount up with wings like eagles, they will run and not get tired, they will walk and not become weary." Isaiah40:31

Day 8: Everyone thinks they know about eagles at least I thought I did. I heard that eagles push their young out of the nest to teach them to fly. You can't always believe what you hear. Eagles build the biggest nests out of all the birds. For many weeks it brings food to the nest for the baby eagles (can I call them eaglets)? Those babies have no worries, everything they need to survive is right there, but when the mother eagle perceives that it's time for the eaglets to fly, things change. The eaglets don't know what's going on, but mom knows it's time. So what does she do? She stops bringing food to them, but puts it in her beak and flies around the nest. She hopes that the babies will be motivated to fly out the nest and take the food out of her beak. I know, I know get to the point.

Ok, think about when you're in a comfortable space/place in your life. You have all you need. There's no room for you to go any further because you're comfortable. You want to stay there forever. Be careful of getting comfortable and staying too long. It's easy to stop dreaming when your belly is full. You don't feel the need to fly at all. Truth is, as long as I was there in that comfortable space, I wasn't fulfilling my own destiny or purpose. I wasn't flying, I was content. Please believe: your greatest prayers are not usually answered in comfort. It took an uncomfortable situation or being hungry to make me get out and fly. Many times in life things are going well and then things change and we wonder why. We wonder what happened. We're caught off guard. Well, I was anyway. (I'm certain you didn't experience this. Take off your masks) But it's in those times God, who knows all things, knows when it's time for us to leave the nest, He allows it to become uncomfortable so that we can move on to our next mission in life, our next hope, next dream, next level. After not realizing this, resisting changes and going through hell, I'm happy to say that I want to become sensitive to when it's time to move that I will move without the turmoil. Don't be stubborn like me that the house has to burn down before you move. Now, I know better. I'm aware of when it starts to happen: Things change and don't make sense, people you've been friends with, in business with or otherwise for years just seem to go crazy and you don't know why.

What I've learned in those moments is that it's time to fly. Business changes, jobs go away, friends break your heart, marriages end, relationships end, and most times all these things are signs that it's time to take a flight to your next level. Nobody likes change, but don't be angry or bitter. Don't be mad with people especially when you know you did right by them, and did all you could for the friend/relationship. I hate to tell you, but this moment isn't about them. It's all about you. If God has allowed you to become so uncomfortable in your situation, then it's time for you to move! Don't be afraid, just fly. What situation is so uncomfortable that you feel you're being starved for what you need? Maybe God is telling you it's time to fly. It's time to fly your own dreams and hopes and goals. Fly for true love and real hope.

Journal writing: What situation is so uncomfortable that you feel you are being starved for what you need? I'm listening. ..

Jonnetta "Jai" Allen

Who Are You?

"But what about you? Who do you say that I am?" Mark 8:29

Day 9: The Scriptures say that Jesus asked Peter, who do you say that I am? What would be the caterpillar's answer to that question? Probably something like this: if you are willing to die to find out or be closed in to come out, then and ONLY then will you know who you truly are! Your YOU now, is not your YOU later. .. Watch!

Journal Writing: Who are you?

_____

_____

_____

_____

_____

_____

_____

_____

_____

_____

Jonnetta "Jai" Allen

Half Empty or Half Full?

Day 10: Most times when people see a glass of water they always want to know whether a person sees it as half empty or half full. Has anyone ever wondered how heavy the glass is? And while in your head right now, please know that the weight absolutely doesn't matter. But it does depend on how long you hold the glass. If you hold it for one minute it's not a problem at all. If you hold it for a day, your arm will feel numb and paralyzed. Either way the weight of the glass NEVER changes.

The longer you hold it the heavier it becomes. Stress and worries are like that glass of water. Think about them for a minute and nothing happens. Think about them a little while longer and they begin to hurt. And if you think about them all day long, you'll feel paralyzed and incapable of doing anything. Remember to put the glass down.

When life hands me lemons I'm making chocolate cake and leave you wondering how I did it...

Journal Writing: How heavy is your glass?

_____

_____

_____

_____

_____

_____

_____

_____

_____

_____

Jonnetta "Jai" Allen

FOCUS

Day 11: One of the most important skills we possess is the ability to FOCUS. When we lose focus we waste time, cause accidents and create struggle. Let go of what will not serve you and hold on to what will increase your success. Tomorrow is a new day. If you wake up you've been afforded another chance. If you don't like where you're headed, turn around.

Not until we are lost, do we begin to find ourselves.

Journal Writing: Have you found you yet?

Jonnetta "Jai" Allen

Transformation

Day 12: When she transformed into a butterfly, the caterpillars spoke not of her beauty, but of her weirdness. They wanted her to change back into what she had always been, only now she has wings.

Journal Writing: What do they want you to turn back into?

Jonnetta "Jai" Allen

I DARE YOU!

Day 13: One of the things I've discovered is that it doesn't matter how long you've been in church, how many people you prayed for or how many scriptures you know, there comes a time when we all find it difficult to trust God. For me it's right now as certain things have gone crazy. I find myself saying, "God where are you? Do you care about the situation I'm in? Do you see what I'm going through? People are asking for prayer, but I need someone to pray for me. Can I get you to be honest? Sometimes you've given all you had, and needed someone to stand in the gap for you. There I find myself and I say, "God are you still there?" I finally heard him say: you got to be able to trust me. Ok, Lord I will trust you. And I began to worship. Even though I can't see you and I can't feel you, God I still trust you. I just know that you're going to make a way for me. I know you wouldn't put me here if you weren't going to bring me out.

God knew that someone else was going through the same thing that I was going through. So I understood that being in this situation was so I would be able to encourage that person whomever they may be. It might even be you reading this right now, and it seems like you can't make it out. You feel like there's no way you can get out of this mess. But you need to know that God is not a respecter of persons. If He brought me out, He can do the same for you. It gets hard sometimes but I still believe. I still trust you. I find myself wondering: God, when will you show up? People are losing jobs, got more bills than money, just had my heart broken, but I'll trust you. You can make a way out of no way. I know you will. You're still here, it's not over. Did you hear me? You're still here, it's not over! I don't know when He's going to do it, but I know He will! Hold on!

__Journal Writing:__ I dare you to praise your way through today.

_____

_____

_____

_____

Jonnetta "Jai" Allen

GOT GOALS?

Day 14: Today, practice as if you are the worst, play as if you are the best. You are a leader and you are the TOTAL PACKAGE. Patience, persistence and perseverance make an unbeatable combination for success. Got goals? Let's meet them. You are enough!

Journal Writing: What are your goals?

Jonnetta "Jai" Allen

Oops.. YOU DROPPED YOUR MASK…YOU WANT IT?

Day 15: Be careful who you pretend to be, you may forget who you really are.

Journal Writing: Who have you been pretending to be? Who do people say that you are? Who are you really?

_____

_____

_____

_____

_____

_____

_____

_____

_____

_____

_____

_____

_____

Jonnetta "Jai" Allen

PAY IT FORWARD

Day 16: Take 15 minutes and sit in front of the mirror. Tell the person looking back at you all the things you needed to hear growing up but never did. Say things like: You are amazing! You mean the world to me. I don't know what I would do if something happened to you. I love you (Say your name). You matter to me. And believe them. Randomly pour those things in to others. Truth is they probably needed to hear them too and didn't. Let's break the cycle and heal.

Journal Writing: Write about your encounters...

Jonnetta "Jai" Allen

YOU ARE BEAUTIFUL!

Day 17: Butterfly, the struggle makes you beautiful. The struggle makes you fly. Spread your wings and be new again. Remember: the struggle makes you beautiful. I don't care what they say or think. The struggle makes you fly. Spread your wings and fly.

Journal Writing: How has your struggle made you beautiful? What has changed?

_____

_____

_____

_____

_____

_____

_____

_____

_____

_____

_____

_____

_____

_____

_____

Jonnetta "Jai" Allen

SELF-INVENTORY

Day 18: Today, spend time reflecting. I know where I am today, but I remember where I was a few months ago physically, mentally, emotionally and spiritually. And as much as I love God I wasn't in a good space. I was questioning everything because nothing made sense. Every time I thought things couldn't get worse, guess what? They did! Good things were happening, but I couldn't appreciate them. The Word says, "If you are faithful over few things, He will make you ruler over much." Losing everything was a bitter pill to swallow. And there was no logical reason why. I had to show God that He could trust me to praise Him with nothing, so that when He gave it back there would be no question what I would do. And trust me, getting it back seemed like it would not happen. Someone told me the things I got back would be better than the things I lost. And in my mind I didn't think that was possible. Besides things were progressively getting worse. A few months later, I'm still here. And I'm better than I've been in a long time.

I learned to just trust God. Take him at His word. God is great! They say it's darkest before dawn, I must say I'm watching the sun rise. All I needed to do was show God that He could trust me. Lord I love you. I magnify your name. You are so worthy to be praised. And even though I doubted and got discouraged, you didn't get upset with me and abandon me. You just kept blessing me even when I failed to acknowledge you. Thank You Lord! To you... Yes you! Be encouraged. It may seem like He's not there, but I promise you He is. The reason you're going through it is because He's equipped you to handle it. Don't give up. God has not forgotten you. Sometimes God allows you to hit rock bottom so you have nowhere to go but up.

Journal Writing: Where's up from here?

_____

_____

_____

_____

Jonnetta "Jai" Allen

SEASON, REACTION AND RESPONSE

Day 19: Let's focus on 3 words: season, reaction and response. Ecclesiastes 3:1 – "to everything there is a season (period of time), and a time (a moment) to every purpose (God given assignment) under the heaven." It's extremely important that we understand that the way we respond in our season (sections of moments), can cause it to be lengthened or shortened. 2 Kings 20: Hezekiah, 39 year old king has just been told by Isaiah to get his house together. His season (sections of moments) was over and he was going to die. When you read it pay attention to the fact that when he hears the message from the prophet Isaiah, he doesn't REACT by having a conversation with Isaiah (the people). Instead he RESPONDS by turning his face to the wall and talks to God. 2 things happen in his prayer. He reminds God of his promise he made to the descendants of David, and he wept (the unspoken words of the heart). Because of Hezekiah's response God RESPONDS by adding 15 years (multiple sections of moments) to his life. STOP REACTING and talking to people who don't have the power to deliver you or change your season (sections of moments) wait on the change. Seasons (sections of moments) come back around if we RESPOND properly rather than REACT. Until then remember 1 Timothy 6:6 "godliness with contentment is great gain."

Journal Writing: What did you experience today? Did you respond or react?

_____

_____

_____

_____

_____

_____

Jonnetta "Jai" Allen

ARE YOU THERE?

Day 20: Being there, means being there... not just physically, but it refers to the connection. Your location is important but again it is not related to geography but the state of that relationship. So if you say you are there for someone, check your location. Are you? When they cried, could you catch their tears or at least hear their voice? Were you a phone call away or did you have to call them back? People say I'm there for you but are they really? The people in your life who are there for you, you will never need to FIND for comfort. Of course there are people who can't be there who live at great distances. But when it comes to support, they should be "close enough" to feel your pain. Being there means being there... Are you? In order to have a good friend, you must first learn to be one...

Journal Writing: Are you a good friend? Do you have good friends? If not, change your circle

Jonnetta "Jai" Allen

THE SECRET IS OUT

"You don't have enough faith. I tell you the truth, if you had faith even as small as a mustard seed, you could say to this mountain, move from here to there, and it will move. Nothing will be impossible." Matthew 17:20

Day 21: What are you struggling with that no one knows about? If you only have faith the size of a mustard seed, you don't have to struggle anymore. You've already been in that place too long. I'm certain it's been rough. But I need you to know that the struggle is over for you.

Journal Writing: What struggles are over? Declare it today!

_____

_____

_____

_____

_____

_____

_____

_____

_____

_____

_____

_____

_____

Jonnetta "Jai" Allen

WHAT'S NEXT?

Day 22: There comes a time when we have to stop looking back and trying to figure out "why". At some point we have to shift our attention to "what's next!" Please tell me:

Journal Writing: What's next for you?

Jonnetta "Jai" Allen

Let GO!

Day 23: When it becomes hard to move on, remember the pain you felt while you were holding on? Healing begins when you let go...

Journal Writing: What are you holding onto? Write it here. Remember you have to let go in order to heal.

Jonnetta "Jai" Allen

WHAT'S GROWING IN YOUR GARDEN?

Day 24: People who have never been in an abusive situation often misunderstand women who are trapped in abusive relationships. Before I ended up there, I was very judgmental of the victims of abuse. I, like many others, thought that only "weak" women stayed in these situations. If someone mistreats you, why not just leave? The reality is, when you are really caught up in abuse, it's simply not that easy. Unfortunately people don't understand the subtle day by-day, moment - by - moment wearing down of the self- esteem that happens. They don't understand the guilt trip that is placed on the abused or the feeling of hopelessness that you won't be able to make it without the abuser.

On the days the guilt works, you fluctuate from feeling like you did something to deserve your abuser being angry to feeling like if you leave him, he will be lost and it's your responsibility to love him back to life. When guilt doesn't work, then fear steps up and kills your will for better. One of the things my abuser used to keep me feeling bad about myself was my past. What I found out after all my wasted efforts was, it was absolutely impossible to have the circumstances of your life change without your heart being changed. The reality is because I had not yet forgiven some people for some mistreatment in my life, I was perpetuating what I hated in my own life. I was filled with resentment, unforgiveness, anger and offense. No matter how badly I wanted my life to be better, all I could really manage to do was come up with temporary changes for long - term issues, like expecting apples from a lemon tree. Unless you can change the root, you will never change the fruit.

Journal Writing: What kind of fruit is growing in your life because of the root? What needs to be planted?

_____

_____

_____

_____

Jonnetta "Jai" Allen

COUNT IT ALL JOY

Day 25: What brings you joy? What dreams have you abandoned because it got too hard or you failed? People will say what you can't do. They will also discourage you from trying to reach your goals. Sadly, even the ones closest to you will say things to hurt you. But whatever you do: DON'T STOP BELIEVING!!! Think about this: every miracle starts with someone telling another what they cannot do.

Journal Writing: What dream was discouraged in you?

Jonnetta "Jai" Allen

HE WILL SUPPLY YOUR NEEDS

"Seek ye first the kingdom of God in his righteousness and all the other things will be added unto you." Matthew 6:33

Day 26: Until God opens the next door for you, praise Him in the hallway! Whatever it is you need God to do let your praise be the down payment. Praise is the Prayer that changes everything.

Journal Writing: What are you praising God on credit for?

Jonnetta "Jai" Allen

HE SPEAKS!

Day 27: Me: Hey God, you got a minute? I need to talk
God: Yeah J, what's up?
Me: You can't get upset with me though... I'm just venting and I need your perspective
God: Alright
Me: Why did you allow so much to happen to me?
God: What do you mean?
Me: well, I grew up in the church and as soon as I was old enough to endure some things, I experienced the worst hurt ever
God: yes
Me: Got married and well, that's a book all by itself. But the turmoil that I'm STILL dealing with.
God: okay
Me: losing a job, homelessness, no income, a part time job that I'm over qualified for and making minimum wage, can't do the things I used to or live the way I used to
God: Hmm mm
Me: staring down the barrel of a gun and it jams. That was traumatizing! Sheesh
God: Alright
Me: and on top of it all, I worked hard to get where I was and it was gone without reasonable explanation. I'm starting all over with nothing. What happened??
God: let me see, the death angel was trying to take you out. I sent an angel who specializes in mechanics to make sure it jammed because it wasn't your time. Traumatizing it may have been but I knew you would be ok. You worked all night that night. Remember?
Me: (humbled) Oh yeah I did
God: you grew up in church and received some of the soundest doctrine there is. You know the word. Not just by memory but it's your life. I let it happen because there's another little girl experiencing that. At the right time, you will meet her and she will need you.
Me: (ashamed) Oh
God: and yes your marriage failed, and the enemy thought he had you. Nobody helped or believed you and that's ok. I kept your mind. I had you. But when she comes to you after nobody believes her, you can help her. And it won't be empathy. It will be: I've been there. I know that feeling and I understand.

Me: (embarrassed) okay
God: losing your job and homelessness. .. I needed you to know what it was to have everything and also have nothing. So when I take you up this time, you will remain humble and also appreciate what you have.
Me: (softly) I see
God: Oh and the reason you're still going through... You didn't ask, but I know you're wondering. The anointing on your life is great. You don't know how great it is. I'm so elated that you've yielded and you're writing. The word that's in you comes across so candidly. You color words so beautifully. You get the message across. Your honesty and candidness sets you apart from them. You show that this walk isn't easy, but it can be done. And you ARE changing lives, whether they tell you or not... I'm telling you. You've already changed lives... Countless. And this book, you have no idea the blessings awaiting you.
Me: I'm sorry Lord
God: Don't worry about it. Just learn to trust me in all things. Good, bad and/or indifferent.
Me: I will trust you
God: And don't ever doubt that my plan for your day is always better than your plan
Me: I won't God. And let me just tell you thank you. Thank you for everything today.
God: J, you're welcome. It was just another day being your God. And I love looking after my children.

Journal Writing: What is He saying to you?

_____

_____

_____

_____

_____

_____

_____

WHO YOU ARE MAKES A DIFFERENCE

Day 28: Who you are makes a difference. Today you need 3 index cards or note cards whichever you choose. You need to identify a person. Write them a note acknowledging them for making a difference in your life. When you present it to them, give them the other 2 index or note cards and instruct them to do the same.

To YOU:
Who you are makes a difference in my life simply because you're reading this. Thank you for surviving and not giving up. Aside from me, I'm certain you make a difference in the lives of others also. Now pay it forward. I just did.

In Love,
Jai

Journal Writing: Write your encounters here.

Living Through the Aftermath

LOVE YOURSELF!

Day 29: Today you have my permission to love on yourself. Write yourself a love letter or poem. Here's mine, I hope it inspires you:

I am a resurrected vessel. Beautiful, moving into another level of wholeness. Excuse me for a second please? I just need to love on me. I awakened with my health, mentally intact (I'm not crazy), emotionally sore and bruised, but guess what, (I still can lift my head), and spiritually free (I can praise God at will) regardless of my current circumstances. So as I took my self- inventory this morning, I happened to notice the beautiful outline of this vessel... Me!

It was then that it dawned on me, I am BEAUTIFUL! I right now am in the process of moving into a place of complete wholeness and complete healing. So I think I reserve the right to love on me for a minute. Ahem... Excuse me but for all the battles that were conquered, all the tears shed, all the negative words that put a damper on my spirit, for the pain that I've overcome, for the growth I managed to experience. I made it and I'm still standing. I'm learning to be the love of my own life right now. And you should too.

Everyone doesn't qualify and/or cannot afford the admission to sit in the VIP section of your soul. So please have your VIP passes and tickets out... I'm choosing me first. No hard feelings, but you don't know my story.

Writing Journal: Declare to love yourself today and everyday forward. What's your story?

_____

_____

_____

_____

_____

_____

_____

Living Through the Aftermath

YOU ARE ENOUGH!

"Ask and it will be given to you, seek and you will find, knock and it will be opened to you. For everyone who asks receives, and he who seeks, finds and to him who knocks it will be opened." Matthew 7:7-8

Day 30: You are enough! The word says: His grace is sufficient for you. Asking is the beginning of receiving. Make sure you don't go to the ocean with a teaspoon. Take a bucket at least, so you don't get laughed at. What are the main reasons you don't ask God for His blessings? Just know, He never makes a promise that He can't keep. Everyone who asks receives. .. Even you! 9 times out of 10, you don't have it because you didn't ask.

Just ask him and watch him do it...

Writing Journal: Ask God for what you want?

_____
_____
_____
_____
_____
_____
_____
_____
_____
_____
_____
_____
_____

Living Through the Aftermath

"The effective, fervent prayers of a righteous man availeth much."
James 5:16

P.U.S.H. (PRAY UNTIL SOMETHINGHAPPENS)

Day 31: I'm going to close this with a prayer and in your writing simply pray your own prayer:

Father God in the name of Jesus, I thank you for the individual reading this right now and went through this whole 30 day journey, asking you God that your will be done in their life. I pray that they submit and allow the Holy Spirit to guide them where they should be at the appointed time. I decree and declare in the name of Jesus that they are the head and not the tail, the lender and not the borrower, above and not beneath. God, your seed is mighty in the earth and you are above average! There will be nothing lacking, broken or missing. I speak wholeness in the name of Jesus and I plead the blood of Jesus over everything that concerns you. It is written that your gifts will make room for you. You already have everything you need. He's waiting on you. You're sitting on it, procrastinating and allowing the enemy to tell you that you need this or that. But I bind the spirit of confusion. You have clear vision, vivid thoughts, humility... You are a child of God. And God you are not a respecter of persons.

You have no favorites. You all your children and the promise belongs to all of us. You don't make us great just for the sake of being great but rather that you can get the glory and someone else's life can be changed. Help the person reading this know that everything they're going through is just adding dimensions and depths to their testimony. How would you know He's a healer if you've never been suck? Help them to keep the faith. For they are destined for great things. Mend their broken hearts, change doubtful minds, touch dying souls but most of all make them whole. Bless them indeed and we will ever be so careful to give you all the praise.
In Jesus Name
Amen

Beloveds, refuse to speak anything other than victory. When you speak to it, it calms just as the sea... Peace be still. He never made a promise that was too good to be true.

Living Through the Aftermath

ABOUT THE AUTHOR

Jonnetta Allen, was born in Jersey City, NJ. She adores God. She is the proud mother of two beautiful children: Tajhinea Nicole & D'maje Elijah. She has had her share of life's ups and downs, but she's still here, living through it, that she might be an encouragement to you. Her first published piece was featured in "Confessions of a Domestic Violence Survivor". She's a wife, mother, singer, actress, aunt and amongst other things, now an author.

www.ingramcontent.com/pod-product-compliance
Lightning Source LLC
Chambersburg PA
CBHW032213040426
42449CB00005B/571